Seeing Myself as God Sees Me

Seven Cycles of Soul Enlightenment

CECILIA B. LOVING

Book sales for North America
and international:
Myrtle Tree Press LLC
376 President Street, Suite 2H
Brooklyn, New York 11231
Phone: 718-596-8019 (toll free 1-800-940-9642)
Fax: 888-583-7086; email orders
(mail to:myrtletreepressllc@gmail.com)

Printed in the United States of America

I SEE GOD AS SILENCE

Seeing Myself as God Sees Me began as a daily meditation. After one of my church members, Elizabeth Walker, commented on how this reflection impacted her, I began to realize its significance. Liz also told me numerous times to publish a book of the meditations that I use on www. spiritmuvmeditation.com. This first book of spiritual contemplation, a personal journal for your own reflection, is how Spirit led me to respond to Liz's request.

So many of our reflections on spiritual growth just focus on manifesting our good. Entering the magnificence of God seeing you also focuses on being one with the Spirit. This divine appointment is divided into seven cycles because seven is a number of spiritual completion. Each cycle is comprised of 21 days because it is well known that we can change our consciousness in 21 days. There are no dates, so that you can begin whenever Spirit calls you to do so. No matter what day it is or what year, life is inviting you to see through the eyes of God, beyond appearances to the absolute good of the kingdom everywhere present.

God is in every word that you write on these pages. Sit in the silence and be blessed by the meditation of simply listening to the Word expressed through you. Begin every entry by at least one minute in the silence. You can use spiritmuvmeditation.com to enter the silence or whatever meditations work best for you. Your listening will evolve as you open your spiritual eyes and see the kingdom of God within, as well as without. The kingdom of God is not simply here or there but is everywhere present (Luke 17:21).

I SEE BY LISTENING

The most important cycle in learning to see ourselves as God sees us is listening. Listening is not as easy as it seems. We have to slow down long enough to hear. Most of us don't want to slow down because we believe that the things that are going on in the world are the most important things in our lives. But if we listen, we will hear Spirit's voice directing our souls to be centered in the kingdom. We will learn that the things of the world will take care of themselves.

We forget that we are spiritual temples of the living God. We forget that we made of Spirit's image and likeness. We spin our wheels moving in so many directions that we fail to embrace our oneness with a universe of absolute good.

How do we listen? We sit comfortably, and close our eyes, and breathe. We listen to our breath, flowing in and out with the harmony of the universe. There is no right or wrong way to meditate, which is another word for listening. Music helps us center in the silence. Certain music is prayer that takes us into our sacred space. Mantras, or truths repeated, are reminders of our oneness with the divine. They also help us enter and remain in the silence. These pages provide mantras. Spirit will also reveal new mantras to your soul in the silence. Write the sacred messages that Spirit unfolds through you.

Cecilia B. Loving

MY LISTENING GOALS

Date

I AM ONE.

Reflect on the significance of your oneness with the Creator. We were at the beginning of the divine creation, empowered with the same ability to co-create with the universe. The Psalmist says be still and know that I am God. Today is the day to stop denying your divine birthright. Realize that you are the co-creative power of omnipotence. Seek first the kingdom within, realizing that all else is added.

Date

Cecilia B. Loving

Date

I AM COVERED IN GOD.

When we are still and realize our divine oneness, we are liberated from even the faintest bit of doubt. In the stillness, we can feel the presence of God, from well beyond our souls to the grace that loves without condition, knowing we are one.

Date

Cecilia B. Loving

_____

_____

_____

_____

_____

_____

_____

_____

_____

_____

_____

_____

_____

_____

_____

_____

_____

Date

I AM STILL.

In this oneness, I am still. I breathe the love that penetrates my soul and emanates throughout my entire being.
I know that whatever I desire is the cosmic consciousness of the universe directing me to be the best that I could ever be.

Date

Cecilia B. Loving

_____

_____

_____

_____

_____

_____

_____

_____

_____

_____

_____

_____

_____

_____

_____

_____

_____

Date

I AM THE SOLUTION I NEED.

God is guiding me and protecting me from every outer vibration that does not contribute to the full expression of God's good. I know what has to be done.
God blesses me with everything I need and more.

Date

Cecilia B. Loving

_____

_____

_____

_____

_____

_____

_____

_____

_____

_____

_____

_____

_____

_____

_____

_____

_____

_____

_____

_____

Date

I STAND ON THE POWER OF PURE POTENTIAL.

~~I am lifted from earth to heaven.~~
I do all things but fail by beginning in the silence.

Date

Cecilia B. Loving

Date

I AM GOD'S FULL EXPRESSION – AND GOD EXPRESSES THROUGH ME FULLY.

I stop trying, and divine ideas are revealed to me.
In each idea, I express as the full power of God.

Date

Cecilia B. Loving

Date

OUR GOD IS REAL.

I center in the awareness that there is an energy,
a force, a power, a presence, a wisdom, a love that forms,
shapes, evolves and expresses as us. Some may call God,
I AM, or Love, or the Universe, or Divine Mind.
Regardless of what we call God – our God is real.

Date

Cecilia B. Loving

_____

_____

_____

_____

_____

_____

_____

_____

_____

_____

_____

_____

_____

_____

_____

_____

_____

_____

Date

I AM A WILLING SERVANT.

This is the heritage of the servants of the Lord, and their
righteousness is from Me, says the Lord.
I let go of my will and instead am willing to listen
and be obedient to Spirit.

Date

Cecilia B. Loving

Date

GOD BREATHES MY SOUL.

I listen to God breathing me as Spirit.
I realize that my soul is a unique expression of God.

_____

_____

_____

_____

_____

_____

_____

_____

_____

_____

_____

_____

_____

_____

_____

_____

_____

Date

Cecilia B. Loving

_____

_____

_____

_____

_____

_____

_____

_____

_____

_____

_____

_____

_____

_____

_____

_____

_____

Date

I AM FREE IN THE MIND OF GOD.

I am immersed in the Mind of God, which is the only liberation from fear, doubt and hopelessness there is.

Date

Cecilia B. Loving

_____

_____

_____

_____

_____

_____

_____

_____

_____

_____

_____

_____

_____

_____

_____

_____

_____

_____

Date

<u>NO WEAPON AGAINST ME PROSPERS.</u>

~~Even when enemies try to destroy us they fall back on swords~~ of their own making. See the arrows that fly before us, past us, below us. No weapon formed against us shall prosper.

_____

_____

_____

_____

_____

_____

_____

_____

_____

_____

_____

_____

_____

_____

_____

_____

Date

Cecilia B. Loving

_____

_____

_____

_____

_____

_____

_____

_____

_____

_____

_____

_____

_____

_____

_____

_____

_____

Date

I AM ETERNAL GOOD.

The scripture says touch not my anointed and do my
prophets no harm. And who are we prophets
but the eternal consciousness of Spirit,
radiating as absolute good in the lives of others.

Cecilia B. Loving

Date

GOD'S LOVE NEVER LEAVES ME.

God is the green pasture of our souls.
God is the quiet water of our hearts.
God is the eternal forgiveness
of love that never leaves nor forsakes us.

Date

Cecilia B. Loving

_____

_____

_____

_____

_____

_____

_____

_____

_____

_____

_____

_____

_____

_____

_____

_____

_____

_____

Date

I SEE GOD.

I see God in the Eden of Divine Mind.
I breathe God in the dew of sweet enlightenment.
I pour God from the river that restores me
throughout eternity.

Cecilia B. Loving

_____

_____

_____

_____

_____

_____

_____

_____

_____

_____

_____

_____

_____

_____

_____

_____

_____

_____

_____

Date

GOD FEEDS ME GOODNESS AND MERCY.

I walked with God on the path of righteousness.
Spirit moved with me, made me surrender,
lifted me above contempt and controversy,
fed me goodness and mercy.

Date

Cecilia B. Loving

Date

I FEAR NO EVIL.

The Lord is my shepherd, the Psalmist sang,
and I saw that I could walk through the valley of death without
a single iota of fear, knowing that God's love
is always with me.

Date

Cecilia B. Loving

_____

_____

_____

_____

_____

_____

_____

_____

_____

_____

_____

_____

_____

_____

_____

_____

_____

_____

_____

_____

Date

I TRIUMPH IN GOD.

If God is for me, then who can be against me.
The battles we think are ours are really the Lord's.

Date

Cecilia B. Loving

_____

_____

_____

_____

_____

_____

_____

_____

_____

_____

_____

_____

_____

_____

_____

_____

_____

Date

I RELEASE THE WORRY OF FEAR.

In righteousness you shall be established;
You shall be far from oppression, for you shall not fear;
And from terror, for it shall not come near you.

Date

Cecilia B. Loving

_____

_____

_____

_____

_____

_____

_____

_____

_____

_____

_____

_____

_____

_____

_____

_____

_____

_____

Date

I AM PERFECT IN GOD.

Even when I am not worthy, You will lift me up into the perfection of who You are.

Date

Cecilia B. Loving

Date

I AM IN GOD.

I will dwell in You forever.
My soul will emanate You from every pore,
molecule and atom of my being.

Cecilia B. Loving

_____

_____

_____

_____

_____

_____

_____

_____

_____

_____

_____

_____

_____

_____

_____

_____

_____

_____

_____

Date

<u>MY DAY IS FILLED WITH MIRACLES.</u>

I see love where there once was fear, harmony where there once were distractions, accomplishment where there once was strife, abundance where I used to see lack.
I see miracles flowing without ceasing.

Date

Cecilia B. Loving

_____

_____

_____

_____

_____

_____

_____

_____

_____

_____

_____

_____

_____

_____

_____

_____

_____

Date

_____

_____

_____

_____

_____

_____

_____

_____

_____

_____

_____

_____

_____

_____

_____

_____

_____

_____

_____

Date

I SEE THROUGH LOVE

Love's light enters my body and heals my soul. Love's light lifts my mind and embraces my heart. Love's light strengthens my spirit and erases my fear. Love's light blesses each organ, each cell, each particle, each limb, each bone, each, muscle, each vein, each ounce, each follicle, each gland of the temple that I call me – and reminds me that it is whole, it is complete, it is radiant, it is strong, it is as it was in the beginning: powerful, sacred and divine.

Love's light centers my mind in the truth that every aspect of my body supports the journey of my soul, the power of my connection, the wisdom of the universe expressing as me. Love's light forgives me from the foundation of my feet, through the legs of my movement, through the knees of my magnificence, through the thighs of my victory, through the creativity of my reproductive center, through the belly of my intuition, through the heart of my goodness, through the throat of my genius, through the eyes of my vision, through the crown of the I AM that I AM. Love's light eases all pain, delivers me from all despair, resolves all worries, fulfills all dreams, reaches all goals, surrenders all longings with a brilliance that never leaves me.

In this cycle of love, I allow love's light to clear my consciousness with the freedom to be who I am and to do what I am called to do.

Cecilia B. Loving

MY GOALS OF LOVE

Date

LOVE FORGIVES ME.

Love's light forgives me.
I am neither limitation nor lack.
I am the fullest expression of love,
the I AM that I AM.

Cecilia B. Loving

Date

THE CHRIST IN ME IS LOVE.

*The love that I am penetrates all discord
and brings perfect peace to all relationships..*

Date

Cecilia B. Loving

_____

_____

_____

_____

_____

_____

_____

_____

_____

_____

_____

_____

_____

_____

_____

_____

_____

_____

Date

LOVE IS THE EXPANSION OF MY TERRITORY.

I give my best and Love does the rest,
expanding my territory with God's grace.

Cecilia B. Loving

Date

DIVINE IDEAS NEVER STOP BLESSING ME.

I will slow down in this moment and breathe in the awareness that divine ideas never stop blessing me and others through me.

Date

Cecilia B. Loving

_____

_____

_____

_____

_____

_____

_____

_____

_____

_____

_____

_____

_____

_____

_____

_____

_____

_____

Date

I AM AWARE OF LOVE BREATHING ME.

*I will sit in a comfortable position, and close my eyes,
and center in the breath of this awareness.*

Date

Cecilia B. Loving

Date

I SEE BEYOND APPEARANCES.

Love is the righteous judgment of all there is.

Date

Cecilia B. Loving

Date

LOVE NEVER STOPS POURING.

I AM more than a conqueror, I am a child of endless favor –
filled with love that never stop pouring.

Date

Cecilia B. Loving

Date

LOVE IGNITES MY SOUL.

Love fills my body with its perfect wholeness, blessing every aspect of my being with energy, strength, compassion, and joy.

Date

Cecilia B. Loving

Date

LOVE BLESSES ME BEYOND BELIEF.

Love fills my mind with divine ideas and gives me the insight, direction and guidance that I need.

Date

Cecilia B. Loving

Date

LOVE LIFTS ME ABOVE THE FRAY.

Love fills my soul with peace, focus and harmony – going before me in ages to come so that I have divine order, good judgment and lasting success.

Cecilia B. Loving

_____
_____
_____
_____
_____
_____
_____
_____
_____
_____
_____
_____
_____
_____
_____

Date

LOVE LIBERATES ME.

Fear frees itself from the appearances that do not see that God is paving a way for me. Limitations lift themselves from the agony of blame – liberating me from pain and shame.

Date

Cecilia B. Loving

_____

_____

_____

_____

_____

_____

_____

_____

_____

_____

_____

_____

_____

_____

_____

_____

_____

_____

_____

Date

LOVE GIVES ME THE MIRACLES I NEED.

Worry releases itself and washes off me like past moments, vanishing into time long gone. Karma, cause and effect bow down to the power of grace.

Date

Cecilia B. Loving

Date

GRACE LOVES ME WITHOUT CONDITION.

Grace cleanses me, and renews me, and refreshes me, and restores me until I am reborn in the womb of love.

Cecilia B. Loving

_____

_____

_____

_____

_____

_____

_____

_____

_____

_____

_____

_____

_____

_____

_____

_____

_____

_____

Date

LOVE HEALS MY BODY.

Love's light enters my body and heals my soul.

Date

Cecilia B. Loving

_____

_____

_____

_____

_____

_____

_____

_____

_____

_____

_____

_____

_____

_____

_____

_____

_____

_____

Date

LOVE LEADS ME INTO SACRED PATHS.

I see ways carved out of no way.

Date

Cecilia B. Loving

Date

LOVE PENETRATES MY BEING.

*Love's light blesses each organ, each cell, each particle, each
limb, each bone, each muscle, each vein, each ounce, each follicle,
each gland of the temple that I call me
– and reminds me that I am the whole being of God.*

Date

Cecilia B. Loving

_____

_____

_____

_____

_____

_____

_____

_____

_____

_____

_____

_____

_____

_____

_____

_____

_____

_____

Date

LOVE CENTERS IN ME.

Love's light centers my mind in the truth that every aspect of my body supports the journey of my soul, the power of divine connection and the wisdom of the universe expressing as me.

Date

Cecilia B. Loving

———————————————————

———————————————————

———————————————————

———————————————————

———————————————————

———————————————————

———————————————————

———————————————————

———————————————————

———————————————————

———————————————————

———————————————————

———————————————————

———————————————————

———————————————————

———————————————————

———————————————————

———————————————————

———————————————————

Date

LOVE IS MY LIGHT OF SALVATION.

Blessed with the salvation of love here and now,
I watch every challenge fall by the wayside.

Date

Cecilia B. Loving

_____

_____

_____

_____

_____

_____

_____

_____

_____

_____

_____

_____

_____

_____

_____

_____

_____

_____

_____

_____

Date

LOVE RADIATES IN MY SOUL.

I am the presence and power of Love reflecting as me.

Date

Cecilia B. Loving

Date

LOVE IS MY GUIDANCE.

*I am the manifestation of love that never stops flowing,
grateful for the way and the truth and the life.*

Date

Cecilia B. Loving

Date

LOVE WINS ALL.

Love's light shows my soul the radiance of now breathing
through every pore of my being, refreshing every opportunity,
giving me the grace to win no matter where I am,
or what I seem, or how I was.

Cecilia B. Loving

_____

_____

_____

_____

_____

_____

_____

_____

_____

_____

_____

_____

_____

_____

_____

_____

_____

_____

_____

Date

Date

I SEE THROUGH RELEASE

I breathe in the power of a healing God, and it breathes in, through and as me. In each breath of healing awareness, I realize that we are one - that there is no black or white, or red or yellow, or brown or beige. We are one family from one village that traveled the world ignited by a God known as absolute good. We share the same breath, the same lungs, the same reproductive process, the same heart, the same senses. We are one in the global recreation of the soul. We are one in the re-connective tissue of the Spirit. We are one in the re-creative consciousness of the mind. This is our planet. These are our lives. Those are our children, and grandchildren. This is our earth. In each breath that I take, I forgive all of the mistakes that we have made, all of the wars that we have started, all of the people that we have failed, all of the wrongs that we have been unable to right, all of the catastrophes that we could have avoided. I forgive the unforgiving bitterness that tends to misdirect our vision to one of hatred rather than love. In each breath, I forgive those who are different than I am, and I embrace the world of endless possibilities. I forgive those who have fallen by the wayside, and I see them lifted up in the grace of unlimited abundance. I see beyond the appearances of popularity and fame to the greatness that resides in every one of us. There is no place where we are that God is not.

Cecilia B. Loving

MY GOALS OF RELEASE

Date

I RELEASE ATTACHMENTS.

I know that whatever I desire is the cosmic consciousness of the universe directing me to enjoy the best that I could ever be. I AM the God that I AM – without attachment, without longing – simply being one.

Date

Cecilia B. Loving

_____

_____

_____

_____

_____

_____

_____

_____

_____

_____

_____

_____

_____

_____

_____

_____

_____

_____

Date

I STOP BEING STAGNATED BY THE FUTURE AND THE PAST.

I release the wilderness of appearances.

Date

Cecilia B. Loving

_____

_____

_____

_____

_____

_____

_____

_____

_____

_____

_____

_____

_____

_____

_____

_____

_____

_____

_____

Date

I MOVE FORWARD.

*I am grateful to move forward and be the infinite blessing
that I am – not tied to anyone or anything but the Spirit
that is my answered prayer, my opened door,
my perfect opportunity.*

Date

Cecilia B. Loving

_____

_____

_____

_____

_____

_____

_____

_____

_____

_____

_____

_____

_____

_____

_____

_____

_____

Date

I RELEASE ALL RESENTMENT.

I let go of hate, shame and blame.

Date

Cecilia B. Loving

Date

I HAVE UNLIMITED GOOD.

My debts are released.

Cecilia B. Loving

_____

_____

_____

_____

_____

_____

_____

_____

_____

_____

_____

_____

_____

_____

_____

_____

_____

_____

_____

_____

_____

Date

MY BURDENS DISAPPEAR.

*I will slow down in this moment and breathe in the
awareness that I am brand new – that all of my burdens
are released and forgiven.*

Cecilia B. Loving

Date

<u>TRUTH BLESSES ME.</u>

My miracles laugh at discord, settle disputes, cleanse distractions, unite divisions, and open my eyes to truth that defies the world of limiting thoughts.

Date

Cecilia B. Loving

Date

I AM GRATEFUL FOR SURRENDER.

I release the mistakes of the past.
I let go of the anxiety of the future.
I reward myself with the awesome awareness of now.

Date

Cecilia B. Loving

_____

_____

_____

_____

_____

_____

_____

_____

_____

_____

_____

_____

_____

_____

_____

_____

_____

Date

I FORGIVE EVERYONE.

*I forgive whatever and whoever has not loved me
and I love them more.*

Date

Cecilia B. Loving

_____

_____

_____

_____

_____

_____

_____

_____

_____

_____

_____

_____

_____

_____

_____

_____

_____

_____

Date

__GOD BLESSES ME.__

I don't care what the future holds because the power of God blesses me, prospers me, and delivers in me in every now moment that there is.

Date

Cecilia B. Loving

Date

I AM FREE FROM LACK.

I am free from needing anything and anyone but God's grace.

Cecilia B. Loving

Date

I AM FREE FROM SIN.

I am free from the sin of believing that I am anything less than I am.

Cecilia B. Loving

_____

_____

_____

_____

_____

_____

_____

_____

_____

_____

_____

_____

_____

_____

_____

_____

_____

_____

Date

MY SOUL IS LOVE'S DIVINE IDEA.

I release fear and allow the holy ghost of good
to fill my heart with perfect bliss.

Date

Cecilia B. Loving

_____

_____

_____

_____

_____

_____

_____

_____

_____

_____

_____

_____

_____

_____

_____

_____

_____

_____

Date

MY SOUL IS FAVORED.

I release the condemnation of ego and worry and sin,
and I rise in the pure power of love,
a love that enriches me
and demonstrates nothing but favor.

Date

Cecilia B. Loving

_____

_____

_____

_____

_____

_____

_____

_____

_____

_____

_____

_____

_____

_____

_____

_____

_____

_____

_____

_____

Date

I STOP GOING THROUGH THE MOTIONS.

I am nothing less than the greatness that I am.

Date

Cecilia B. Loving

Date

I RELEASE ALL RESENTMENT.

I let go of hate, shame and blame.

Date

Cecilia B. Loving

Date

I LET GO AND LET GOD.

I hold on to no one and nothing but God.
All the rest is none of my business.

Date

Cecilia B. Loving

_____

_____

_____

_____

_____

_____

_____

_____

_____

_____

_____

_____

_____

_____

_____

_____

_____

Date

PEACE IS MY INFINITE POWER.

Peace heals the world.
Peace releases judgment.
Peace radiates love without fear.

Cecilia B. Loving

_____

_____

_____

_____

_____

_____

_____

_____

_____

_____

_____

_____

_____

_____

_____

_____

_____

_____

Date

I BREATHE NEW AWARENESS.

I will slow down in this moment and
breathe in the awareness that love heals through me,
that love blesses us all through the power of harmony.

Date

Cecilia B. Loving

Date

THE UNIVERSE CONSPIRES TO HELP ME.

Love removes despair. Love cures disease.
Love cleanses the toxins.

Date

Cecilia B. Loving

_____

_____

_____

_____

_____

_____

_____

_____

_____

_____

_____

_____

_____

_____

_____

_____

_____

_____

_____

_____

Date

THE TRUTH SETS ME FREE.

Silence lifts me into new realms of perfection, heals me with a new armor of resurrection, restores me with a new acceptance of favor fulfilling me with new dreams, triumphs, victories and successes of surrendering to the truth of the kingdom within.

Date

Cecilia B. Loving

_____

_____

_____

_____

_____

_____

_____

_____

_____

_____

_____

_____

_____

_____

_____

_____

_____

_____

Date

Seeing Myself as God Sees Me: *Seven Cycles of Spiritual Enlightenment*

_____

_____

_____

_____

_____

_____

_____

_____

_____

_____

_____

_____

_____

_____

_____

_____

_____

_____

_____

Date

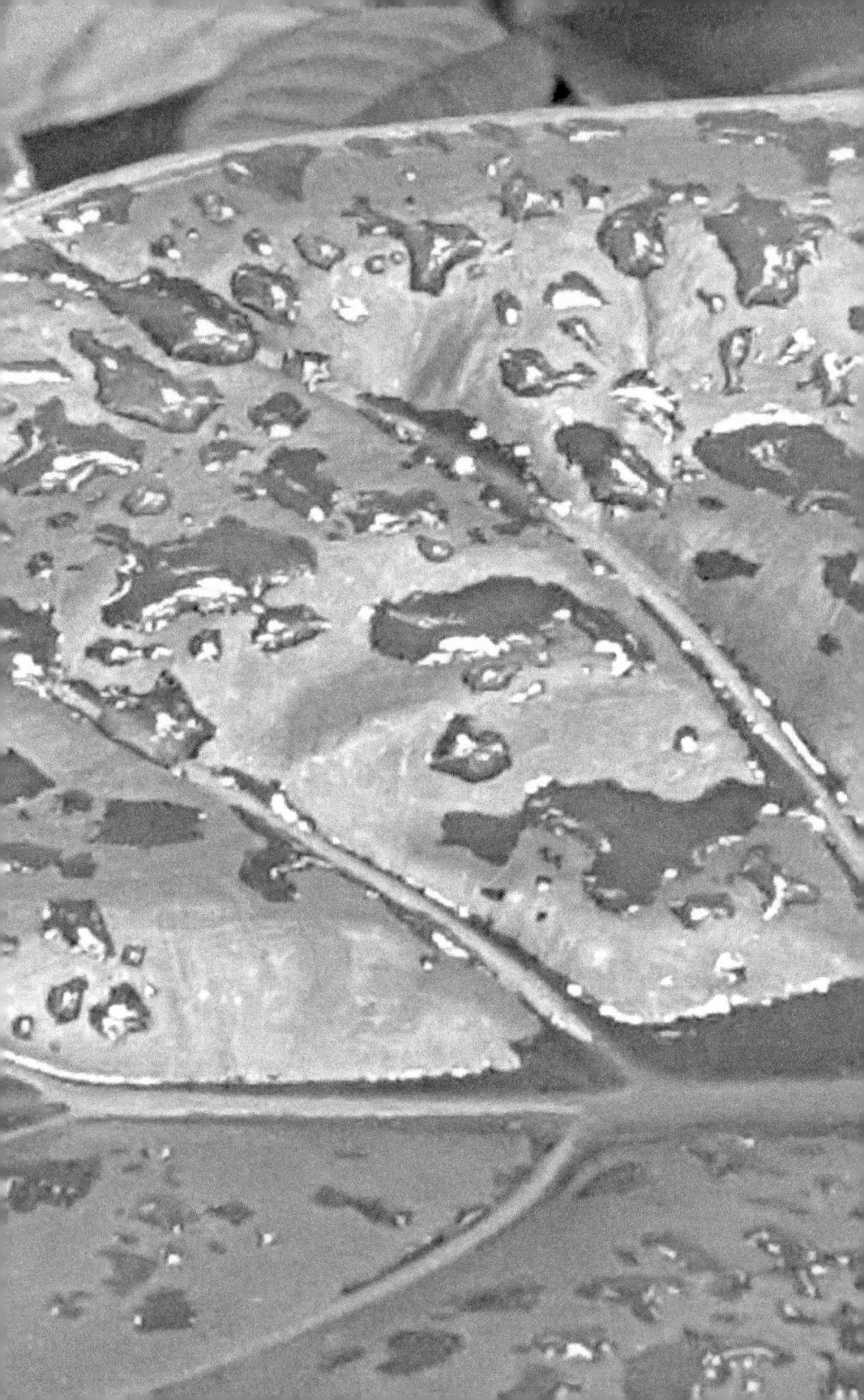

I SEE MANNA EVERYWHERE

The soul is fed by divine substance, the food of God that never stops feeding us the regenerative source of absolute good. Manna is the good, the inexhaustible supply that feeds us the spiritual sustenance of loving grace, always providing the holy nutrition that we want – always there when we need inner guidance – always pouring the fulfillment to our deepest desires – always delivering the answers to our daily prayers.

Manna is the divine presence of fulfillment. We always have what we need, when we need it.

We may not believe that we will receive what the universe desires to give, but it is always here – waiting to bless us.

When we listen, we hear the soul's insistence that we can open our hearts to receive the manna of life – God's good raining, pouring down on us from endless directions.

Listening allows us to receive a fresh supply of the kingdom's riches, to revel in the good of the universe pouring, raining down on us. When we listen, we know that we can stop allowing the fear of lack to prevail because unlimited supply continues to shower us with manna. All we have to do is take what we need, when we need it. Our supply is always here.

Cecilia B. Loving

MY GOALS OF SUPPLY

Date

MANNA FEEDS ME WHATEVER I NEED

Manna feeds me the spiritual sustenance of loving grace, the sweetness of absolute good, always providing the nutrition that we want – always there when we need it – always pouring the fulfillment to our deepest desires – always delivering the answers to daily prayers.

Date

Cecilia B. Loving

_____

_____

_____

_____

_____

_____

_____

_____

_____

_____

_____

_____

_____

_____

_____

_____

_____

Date

MY PROSPERITY NEVER CEASES TO POUR.

I AM the manna of love's substance feeding.

Date

Cecilia B. Loving

Date

I AM TRIUMPH.

I AM the wellspring of love's pure joy. I AM the pool of love's angels stirring. I AM the triumph of love's freedom liberating. I AM the manna of love's substance feeding.

Cecilia B. Loving

Date

MANNA FEEDS US WITH GRACE.

Breathe the breath of you loving this moment –
not asking the universe for anyone or anything,
simply being fed by the manna of grace.

Cecilia B. Loving

_____

_____

_____

_____

_____

_____

_____

_____

_____

_____

_____

_____

_____

_____

_____

_____

_____

_____

_____

_____

Date

MY GOOD IS HERE.

I stop waiting to achieve that which I already have.
I stop spinning my wheels of resistance and see that I have
already arrived. In the stillness, I am liberated from even the
faintest second of doubt.

Date

Cecilia B. Loving

Date

I AM THE WHOLE BEING OF GOD

I am the whole being of God – not part of God, not a piece of God, not a bit – or a fragment – or a reduction – or a stepchild – or an unhealed, poorly attended creature but the whole being of all that Spirit is.

Date

Cecilia B. Loving

_____

_____

_____

_____

_____

_____

_____

_____

_____

_____

_____

_____

_____

_____

_____

_____

_____

_____

_____

Date

I AM NOT LIMITED BY APPEARANCES.

What appeared to be an affliction blesses me. Beyond what looked like good and evil is the whole being of God always healing, prospering, strengthening, and transforming me.

Date

Cecilia B. Loving

Date

I REACH THE UNSPOILED CLEARING.

This is what I will eat and drink and wear: manna as lasting as dew, and water that rises from rocks, and hems that touch the unlimited well of wholeness and strength.

Date

Cecilia B. Loving

Date

MANNA CALMS MY SOUL

In the consciousness of the I AM,
I am the prosperity of endless manna and living water.

_____

_____

_____

_____

_____

_____

_____

_____

_____

_____

_____

_____

_____

_____

Date

Cecilia B. Loving

_____

_____

_____

_____

_____

_____

_____

_____

_____

_____

_____

_____

_____

_____

_____

_____

_____

_____

Date

I FEED THE SPIRIT.

I get the right rest in the arms of God. I breathe the right breath through lasting meditations. I stretch the right moves in worship and dance. I eat the right foods that feed Spirit rather than flesh.

Date

Cecilia B. Loving

_____

_____

_____

_____

_____

_____

_____

_____

_____

_____

_____

_____

_____

_____

_____

_____

_____

_____

Date

I BREATHE IN GOD.

I will slow down in this moment and breathe in the awareness that God is real, that I am my best me – not ruled by sugar, excess or processed food. I exercise and sleep and drink the water of absolute good.

Date

Cecilia B. Loving

Date

DIVINE MIND DIRECTS MY COURSE.

*I am the healing power of victory realizing
that divine mind, soul and body are my birthright.*

Cecilia B. Loving

_____

_____

_____

_____

_____

_____

_____

_____

_____

_____

_____

_____

_____

_____

_____

_____

_____

_____

Date

MANNA LIFTS ME FROM MY MAT OF AFFLICTION.

I am more than healed, more than well, more than renewed, more than changed, more than restored, more than transformed, more lifted than from the pool of Bethesda, I am the whole being of God expressing as the absolute goodness of me.

Date

Cecilia B. Loving

Date

I RECLAIM MY LIFE.

Today, I reclaim my life. I re-chart my course. I re-acknowledge my good. I stand up in the faith that I live, move and have my being in the regenerative source of life.

Date

Cecilia B. Loving

_____

_____

_____

_____

_____

_____

_____

_____

_____

_____

_____

_____

_____

_____

_____

_____

_____

_____

Date

CHRIST IS MY SUPPLY.

I am the bread of life.

Date

Cecilia B. Loving

Date

GOD SEES ME AS ENDLESS SUPPLY.

God sees me as inexhaustible supply everywhere present, pouring through me with prosperity and abundance.

Cecilia B. Loving

Date

I SEE THE ANSWERS TO MY PRAYERS.

I and the Father are one. I and the Mother are one.
I and the Divine Idea of endless abundance and eternal
wholeness and loving creativity are one.

Date

Cecilia B. Loving

_____

_____

_____

_____

_____

_____

_____

_____

_____

_____

_____

_____

_____

_____

_____

_____

_____

_____

Date

MY PROSPERITY NEVER CEASES TO POUR.

I AM the manna of love's substance feeding.

Cecilia B. Loving

_____

_____

_____

_____

_____

_____

_____

_____

_____

_____

_____

_____

_____

_____

_____

_____

_____

_____

Date

I LIVE IN GOD, THROUGH GOD AND AS GOD.

The creative consciousness of the universe anoints me with the abundance of powerful ideas, and I surrender to the good work that God does as me.

Date

Cecilia B. Loving

_____

_____

_____

_____

_____

_____

_____

_____

_____

_____

_____

_____

_____

_____

_____

_____

_____

_____

_____

Date

I AM ALL GOOD YET TO BE.

I am the shape of all good that has ever been,
and all good yet to be.

Date

Cecilia B. Loving

Date

EVERY MOMENT BLESSES ME.

Today's silence blesses me, favors me, restores me, and fulfills God in every breath, every moment, every heartbeat.

Date

Cecilia B. Loving

_____

_____

_____

_____

_____

_____

_____

_____

_____

_____

_____

_____

_____

_____

_____

_____

_____

Date

Date

I SEE THROUGH THE WORD

Listening to the Spirit and learning how it informs the soul requires study. Scripture, spiritual books, classes, groups, online materials, all resources should be used.

The Word is power.

The Word is confirmation.

The Word is truth.

Christ consciousness says I AM the Word. In the beginning, I was everything. I rise in the decrees of all that is. I choose no one but everyone. I sow the seeds of endless rewards. AUM is my name.

When we were created in the image and likeness of God, we were given the gift of words so strong they named the beasts of the fields, the birds of the air, and the fish of the sea – and they were.

The prophets tell us that we shall decree a thing and make it so. Every utterance spoken from our mouths is a gift. Today we realize the unlimited bounty of this gift and we bestow it on all who are, or ever were. We engage in the power of the Word by studying the Word.

Cecilia B. Loving

MY GOALS OF SPEAKING TRUTH TO POWER

Date

I AM ALL GOOD YET TO BE.

I am the shape of all good that has ever been,
and all good yet to be.

Cecilia B. Loving

_____

_____

_____

_____

_____

_____

_____

_____

_____

_____

_____

_____

_____

_____

_____

_____

_____

_____

Date

I RECLAIM MY LIFE.

Today, I reclaim my life through the study of the Word.
I re-chart my course.
I re-acknowledge my good. I stand up in the faith that I
live, move and have my being in the Word.

Date

Cecilia B. Loving

_____

_____

_____

_____

_____

_____

_____

_____

_____

_____

_____

_____

_____

_____

_____

_____

_____

_____

Date

I AFFIRM MY GOOD.

I speak beyond appearances through words that imbue me with favor.

Date

Cecilia B. Loving

_____

_____

_____

_____

_____

_____

_____

_____

_____

_____

_____

_____

_____

_____

_____

_____

_____

_____

Date

I ABIDE IN THE WORD.

I affirm the power and accept a new consciousness of good.

Date

Cecilia B. Loving

_____

_____

_____

_____

_____

_____

_____

_____

_____

_____

_____

_____

_____

_____

_____

_____

_____

Date

I SPEAK WORDS OF MAGNIFICENCE.

I speak words of faith that liberate me in magnificence.

Cecilia B. Loving

_____

_____

_____

_____

_____

_____

_____

_____

_____

_____

_____

_____

_____

_____

_____

_____

_____

_____

_____

Date

THE WORD LIFTS ME ABOVE APPEARANCES.

*I speak the truth beyond appearances in the sanctuary
of perfect peace.*

Date

Cecilia B. Loving

Date

EVERY WORD BLESSES ME.

Every Word blesses me, favors me, fulfills God in every breath, every moment, every heartbeat.

Date

Cecilia B. Loving

_____

_____

_____

_____

_____

_____

_____

_____

_____

_____

_____

_____

_____

_____

_____

_____

_____

_____

Date

WORDS FEED ME WITH SPIRIT.

Words anoint me with lasting meditations. I partake of words that feed with Spirit rather than flesh.

Cecilia B. Loving

Date

I AFFIRM THE POWER OF GRACE.

I speak the truth that karma falls by the wayside because grace is all good.

Date

Cecilia B. Loving

_____

_____

_____

_____

_____

_____

_____

_____

_____

_____

_____

_____

_____

_____

_____

_____

_____

Date

I HAVE NOTHING TO HIDE.

*I affirm the power and presence of the kingdom of God, here
and now, and I rise in the realization
that I have nothing to hide.*

Date

Cecilia B. Loving

_____

_____

_____

_____

_____

_____

_____

_____

_____

_____

_____

_____

_____

_____

_____

_____

_____

Date

I AM REFRESHED BY WORDS OF REBIRTH.

The solution I need is already here.

Date

Cecilia B. Loving

_____

_____

_____

_____

_____

_____

_____

_____

_____

_____

_____

_____

_____

_____

_____

_____

_____

_____

_____

Date

I AFFIRM NEW HEALING.

My prayers have already been answered.

Date

Cecilia B. Loving

_____

_____

_____

_____

_____

_____

_____

_____

_____

_____

_____

_____

_____

_____

_____

_____

_____

_____

_____

Date

I AM THE CONSCIOUSNESS OF CHRIST.

I have everything that I need.

Date

Cecilia B. Loving

_____

_____

_____

_____

_____

_____

_____

_____

_____

_____

_____

_____

_____

_____

_____

_____

_____

Date

GOD BLESSES ALL THAT I AM.

I am made fresh in the new awareness that my Mother and Father God are always blessing me, in every crack and crevice of my existence.

Date

Cecilia B. Loving

Date

I AM A TEMPLE OF THE LIVING GOD.

No matter how old I am, how much I judge myself, how much I have felt the condemnation of others, I bless my temple of the living God.

Date

Cecilia B. Loving

Date

I ANSWER TO NO ONE BUT GOD.

I take the unbeaten path.

Date

Cecilia B. Loving

_____

_____

_____

_____

_____

_____

_____

_____

_____

_____

_____

_____

_____

_____

_____

_____

_____

_____

Date

GOD SEES ME AS SPECTACULAR.

I stretch beyond who I thought I was, and I welcome who I am.

_____

_____

_____

_____

_____

_____

_____

_____

_____

_____

_____

_____

_____

_____

_____

_____

_____

_____

_____

_____

Date

Cecilia B. Loving

Date

GOD SEES ME AS PERFECT.

I am centered in the light in me.

Date

Cecilia B. Loving

Date

GOD SEES ME AS A GOOD THING.

I see a new opening beyond my limits,
and a new me enjoying a good thing.

Date

Cecilia B. Loving

_____

_____

_____

_____

_____

_____

_____

_____

_____

_____

_____

_____

_____

_____

_____

_____

Date

GOD SEES ME AS LOVING EXPRESSION.

I am the light of the world.

Date

Cecilia B. Loving

_____

_____

_____

_____

_____

_____

_____

_____

_____

_____

_____

_____

_____

_____

_____

_____

_____

_____

Date

GOD SEES ME AS AWESOME.

*I am the power of Spirit recreating its awesome energy
in, as and through me.*

Date

Cecilia B. Loving

Date

Date

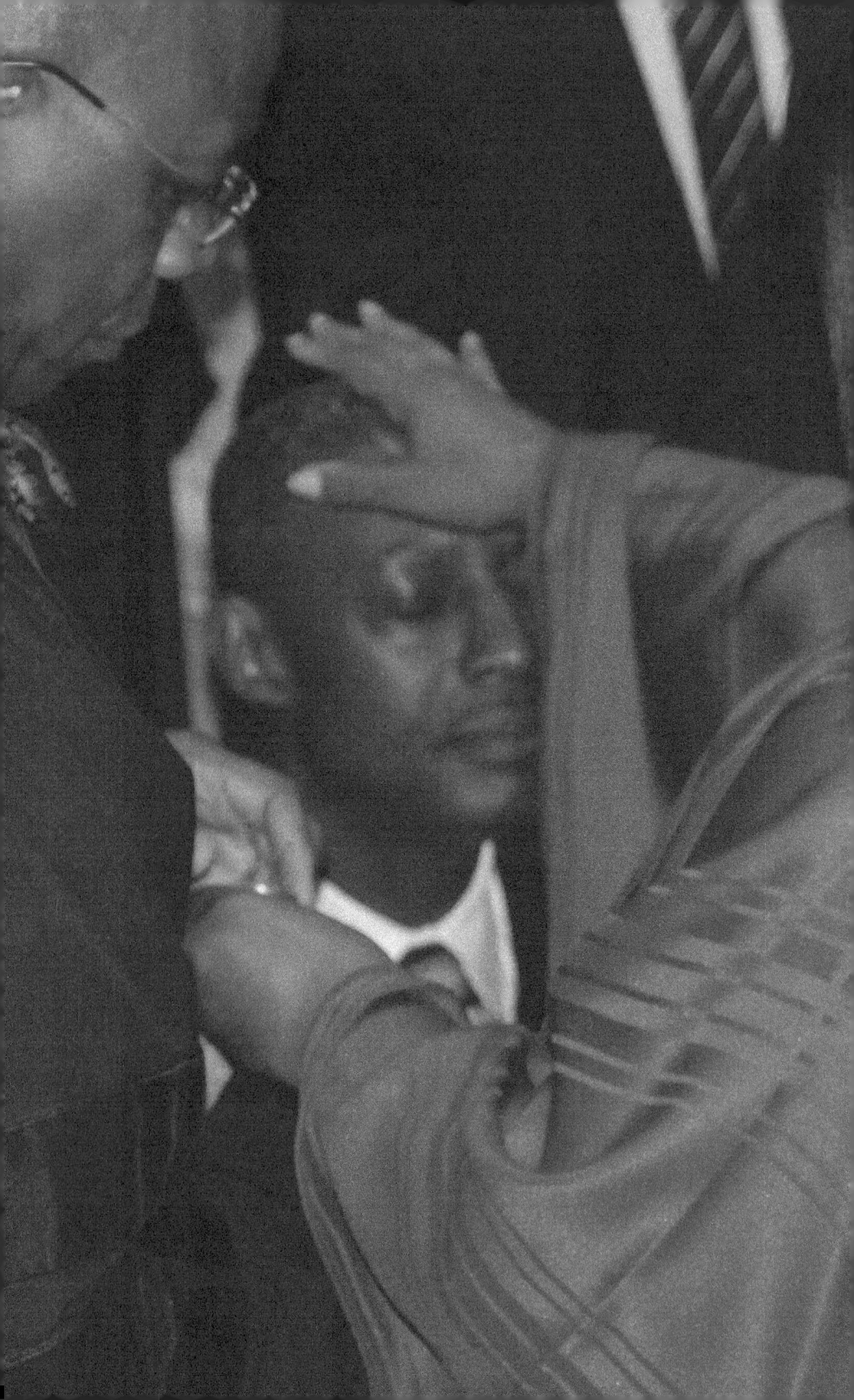

I SEE THROUGH OBEDIENCE

We are tapping into the power of Spirit, a power that is always available as us - to reward us, to strengthen us, to uplift us, to guide us, to prosper us.

Spirit is not a power that we have to beg for: it expresses through and as our very being. Obedience is our ability to choose. We have the power to choose to be well. We have the power to choose to succeed. We have the ability to choose to be wealthy. We have the power to choose to be strong. We have the power to choose to be smart. We have the power to choose to feel great about being great.

Obedience to Spirit guarantees our good.

The Spirit in us is not one of timidity or fear but a Spirit of Power. The sooner we recognize our power, the sooner we accomplish our goals; the sooner we step up to the plate and do what we were called here in this lifetime to do, the sooner we make the world a better place; the sooner we evolve and grow into a completely new existence - one that fully recognizes the gods that we are.

We are the co-creators of our own reality. The Inexhaustible Supply of the Universe is within us, awaiting our obedience. We are Source in a physical Body but the Spirit in which we dwell is far greater than we could ever imagine. No one has the power to deprive us of anything but ourselves.

Cecilia B. Loving

MY GOALS OF OBEDIENCE

Date

I AM OBEDIENT TO SPIRIT.

Spirit always reveals the work that we are appointed to do –
the reason we are here in this existence, at this time and
appointed place. But we have to be obedient
to its divine guidance.

Date

Cecilia B. Loving

_____

_____

_____

_____

_____

_____

_____

_____

_____

_____

_____

_____

_____

_____

_____

_____

_____

_____

_____

_____

Date

I AM FORMED IN THE MIND OF GOD.

I accomplish more than has ever been realized through obedience, more than has ever been imagined.

Date

Cecilia B. Loving

_____

_____

_____

_____

_____

_____

_____

_____

_____

_____

_____

_____

_____

_____

_____

_____

_____

_____

Date

I REAP GOD'S GOOD THROUGH OBEDIENCE.

I step out of the temporary holding patterns of life and start being better than I have ever anticipated.

_____

_____

_____

_____

_____

_____

_____

_____

_____

_____

_____

_____

_____

_____

_____

_____

Date

Cecilia B. Loving

_____

_____

_____

_____

_____

_____

_____

_____

_____

_____

_____

_____

_____

_____

_____

_____

_____

_____

_____

Date

OBEDIENCE OPENS DOORS WITH EASE.

*Not only each day, but each moment blesses me with a
gift to start anew – to do something greater than
anything that has ever been done
simply by listening to Spirit.*

Date

Cecilia B. Loving

_____

_____

_____

_____

_____

_____

_____

_____

_____

_____

_____

_____

_____

_____

_____

_____

_____

_____

_____

Date

GOD SEES ME AS PURE WISDOM.

My light cannot be hidden under a bushel.
In obedience, I give light to all in the house.

Cecilia B. Loving

_____

_____

_____

_____

_____

_____

_____

_____

_____

_____

_____

_____

_____

_____

_____

_____

_____

_____

Date

GOD SEES ME AS DISCIPLINE.

With courage of discipline, I am lifted.

Date

Cecilia B. Loving

_____

_____

_____

_____

_____

_____

_____

_____

_____

_____

_____

_____

_____

_____

_____

_____

_____

_____

Date

GOD SEES ME AS A GOOD THING.

When I am obedient, I see a new opening beyond my limits,
and a new me enjoying a good thing.

Cecilia B. Loving

Date

GOD SEES ME AS AN INSTRUMENT OF CHANGE.

I stretch beyond who I thought I was,
and I welcome who I am.

Cecilia B. Loving

_____

_____

_____

_____

_____

_____

_____

_____

_____

_____

_____

_____

_____

_____

_____

_____

_____

_____

_____

Date

GOD SEES ME AS PERFECT.

When I am obedient, God's light shines through all of my perfection.

_____

_____

_____

_____

_____

_____

_____

_____

_____

_____

_____

_____

_____

_____

_____

_____

_____

_____

Date

Cecilia B. Loving

_____

_____

_____

_____

_____

_____

_____

_____

_____

_____

_____

_____

_____

_____

_____

_____

_____

_____

_____

_____

Date

THROUGH OBEDIENCE, I AM BLESSED BEYOND THE BOUNDARIES OF LIMITATION.

*I depart from the boundaries of what I knew
to what I know works.*

Date

Cecilia B. Loving

_____

_____

_____

_____

_____

_____

_____

_____

_____

_____

_____

_____

_____

_____

_____

_____

_____

_____

Date

I START ANEW.

I stop trying to fit the pattern of what I am accustomed to doing and am obedient to Spirit.

Cecilia B. Loving

Date

<u>LOVE BREATHES THROUGH DISCIPLINE.</u>

My battle is won through the obedience of change.

Date

Cecilia B. Loving

Date

I AM UNLIMITED IN CHRIST.

I walk the water of obedience to faith.

Date

Cecilia B. Loving

_____

_____

_____

_____

_____

_____

_____

_____

_____

_____

_____

_____

_____

_____

_____

_____

_____

_____

_____

Date

I AM FORMED IN THE ARMS OF GOD.

*God shapes and forms my vision
through the power of new habits.*

Cecilia B. Loving

Date

GOD IS MY OBEDIENCE.

I fly in Infinite Possibility.

Date

Cecilia B. Loving

_____

_____

_____

_____

_____

_____

_____

_____

_____

_____

_____

_____

_____

_____

_____

_____

_____

_____

Date

I AM NOT AFRAID TO BE OBEDIENT.

I soar in Everlasting Power.

Date

Cecilia B. Loving

_____

_____

_____

_____

_____

_____

_____

_____

_____

_____

_____

_____

_____

_____

_____

_____

_____

_____

Date

SPIRIT MOVES IN ME WITH
THE FREEDOM OF DISCIPLINE.

I dance in Perfect Harmony.

Cecilia B. Loving

Date

THANK YOU GOD FOR RENEWED FAITH IN DISCIPLINE AND OBEDIENCE.

I release the mistakes of disobedience.
I reward myself with training daily.

Date

Cecilia B. Loving

_____

_____

_____

_____

_____

_____

_____

_____

_____

_____

_____

_____

_____

_____

_____

_____

_____

_____

_____

Date

THANK YOU GOD FOR ALLOWING ME TO SEE YOU.

Each moment opens a new awareness
of the greater good flowing in, as and through me.

Date

Cecilia B. Loving

_____

_____

_____

_____

_____

_____

_____

_____

_____

_____

_____

_____

_____

_____

_____

_____

_____

Date

I SURRENDER TO GOD'S DIRECTION.

*Nothing and no one can interfere with my success,
not even me.*

Date

Cecilia B. Loving

Date

I WALK IN OBEDIENCE TO GOD.

The first step that I took upon the water, I could feel each wave of hopelessness rise and fall like the nothingness of fresh ethers drawn across the horizon of absolute good.

Date

Cecilia B. Loving

_____

_____

_____

_____

_____

_____

_____

_____

_____

_____

_____

_____

_____

_____

_____

_____

_____

Date

_____

_____

_____

_____

_____

_____

_____

_____

_____

_____

_____

_____

_____

_____

_____

_____

_____

_____

_____

_____

Date

I SEE GOD WITH GRATITUDE

We realize God's good through gratitude, which is the highest praise of God. When we listen to the still, small voice of God always speaking as us, we realize that we have a lot to be thankful for. We can see God by recognizing the divine presence in all things. We can see God seeing us through the opportunities that give us what we need to succeed. We can give thanks for the air that we breathe, the space that we take up, the comfort of our homes, the food that we have to eat, the provision of our jobs.

Praise invites more than mere witness, it gives us the intelligence to move out of the way and allow God's good to take shape. Spirit blesses us with the experience that we need in perfect divine order, as well as the unique gifts and talents that best equip us to manifest the good work that we are created to do.

By giving thanks, we can stop asking what the future has in store for us, and instead give thanks for what we have in store for the future. Through the second sight of gratitude, I see God guiding me to experiences that I never could have imagined.

I turn on and tune into the absolute good of the universe by simply being grateful, and see God's blessings multiply as me.

Cecilia B. Loving

MY GOALS OF GRATITUDE

Date

I AM GRATEFUL THAT MY SOUL TEACHES ME.

The knowledge and wisdom of the universe is a wellspring within me, and I access it anytime I need.

Date

Cecilia B. Loving

_____

_____

_____

_____

_____

_____

_____

_____

_____

_____

_____

_____

_____

_____

_____

_____

_____

_____

_____

Date

I AM GRATEFUL THAT LOVE BREATHES
THROUGH EVERY PORE OF MY BEING.

My battle is won.

Date

Cecilia B. Loving

_____

_____

_____

_____

_____

_____

_____

_____

_____

_____

_____

_____

_____

_____

_____

_____

Date

I AM GRATEFUL TO BE REBORN IN THE GREATNESS OF WHO I AM.

The infinite light of health glows through every organ and cell of my being.

Date

Cecilia B. Loving

_____

_____

_____

_____

_____

_____

_____

_____

_____

_____

_____

_____

_____

_____

_____

_____

_____

_____

_____

Date

I AM GRATEFUL THAT I FEEL GOD'S FRESH ANOINTING.

*I wear the crown of lasting faith and fulfill
the triumph of eternal grace.*

Date

Cecilia B. Loving

_____

_____

_____

_____

_____

_____

_____

_____

_____

_____

_____

_____

_____

_____

_____

_____

_____

_____

Date

I AM GRATEFUL THAT DIVINE ORDER IS
BETTER THAN LUCK.

You are who I need to meet,
and I am your answered prayer.

Date

Cecilia B. Loving

Date

I AM GRATEFUL THAT LOVE ORDERS MY AFFAIRS.

I walk through the promise of new doors, wade through the river of new bliss, cross the threshold of magnificent deliverance.

_____

_____

_____

_____

_____

_____

_____

_____

_____

_____

_____

_____

_____

_____

_____

_____

Date

Cecilia B. Loving

_____

_____

_____

_____

_____

_____

_____

_____

_____

_____

_____

_____

_____

_____

_____

_____

_____

_____

_____

_____

_____

Date

I AM GRATEFUL THAT MY GOOD HAS ALREADY TAKEN SHAPE.

In our oneness, I am unconditional love.

Date

Cecilia B. Loving

_____

_____

_____

_____

_____

_____

_____

_____

_____

_____

_____

_____

_____

_____

_____

_____

_____

_____

Date

I AM GRATEFUL THAT DOUBTS DISAPPEAR.

*God heals and anoints every cell, every molecule,
every atom of my body.*

Date

Cecilia B. Loving

_____

_____

_____

_____

_____

_____

_____

_____

_____

_____

_____

_____

_____

_____

_____

_____

_____

_____

Date

I AM GRATEFUL THAT NOTHING CAN STOP ME FROM EXPRESSING GOD'S GOOD.

Anything less than Spirit leaves me.

_____

_____

_____

_____

_____

_____

_____

_____

_____

_____

_____

_____

_____

_____

_____

_____

_____

Date

Cecilia B. Loving

_____

_____

_____

_____

_____

_____

_____

_____

_____

_____

_____

_____

_____

_____

_____

_____

_____

_____

Date

I AM GRATEFUL THAT LOVE NEVER FAILS.

*What I believed I lost is found in the open door
of eternal creation.*

Date

Cecilia B. Loving

_____

_____

_____

_____

_____

_____

_____

_____

_____

_____

_____

_____

_____

_____

_____

_____

_____

Date

I AM GRATEFUL THAT I KEEP THE CENTER OF THE "I" EMPTY.

The desires deepest in my heart are prayers that were answered before I was.

Date

Cecilia B. Loving

_____

_____

_____

_____

_____

_____

_____

_____

_____

_____

_____

_____

_____

_____

_____

_____

_____

_____

Date

I AM GRATEFUL THAT I AM REALIZED POTENTIAL.

God is in us the same as God is in grace.

Cecilia B. Loving

_____

_____

_____

_____

_____

_____

_____

_____

_____

_____

_____

_____

_____

_____

_____

_____

_____

_____

_____

_____

Date

I AM GRATEFUL THAT GOD SEES ME AS VICTORY.

God sees me as the deliverance of success.
I see God seeing me as victory.

Date

Cecilia B. Loving

_____

_____

_____

_____

_____

_____

_____

_____

_____

_____

_____

_____

_____

_____

_____

_____

_____

_____

_____

Date

I AM GRATEFUL THAT I AM COVERED WITH MIRACLES.

I rise from every transgression.

Cecilia B. Loving

_____

_____

_____

_____

_____

_____

_____

_____

_____

_____

_____

_____

_____

_____

_____

_____

_____

_____

Date

I AM GRATEFUL THAT GRACE SURROUNDS ME
IN PERFECT WHOLENESS.

I breathe in the breath of perfect health and in each breath,
God breathes me – as the flow of freedom from all pain,
transformation from all that is not wholeness expressing as me.

Date

Cecilia B. Loving

Date

I AM GRATEFUL THAT PEACE WILL REIGN.

God is all that I AM, the fulfillment of each breath that I take, the foundation of the ground beneath my feet, the divine illumination that shines as the kingdom within.

Date

Cecilia B. Loving

_____

_____

_____

_____

_____

_____

_____

_____

_____

_____

_____

_____

_____

_____

_____

_____

_____

_____

_____

Date

I AM GRATEFUL THAT I STOP
HOLDING BACK MY BEST.

*I AM the power of God expressing through me
right where I am.*

Date

Cecilia B. Loving

_____

_____

_____

_____

_____

_____

_____

_____

_____

_____

_____

_____

_____

_____

_____

_____

_____

_____

_____

Date

I AM GRATEFUL THAT I STOP DENYING MY GOOD.

Thank you God for allowing me to be the miracle that you are, manifesting the love of your light, the health of your wholeness, the energy of your ideas, the joy of your spirit, the vibrancy of your unlimited greatness.

Date

Cecilia B. Loving

_____

_____

_____

_____

_____

_____

_____

_____

_____

_____

_____

_____

_____

_____

_____

_____

_____

_____

_____

_____

_____

Date

I AM GRATEFUL THAT I STOP WASTING ENERGY.

I am grateful to move forward and be the infinite blessing that I am – not tied to anyone or anything but the Spirit that is my answered prayer, my opened door, my perfect opportunity.

Cecilia B. Loving

_____

_____

_____

_____

_____

_____

_____

_____

_____

_____

_____

_____

_____

_____

_____

_____

_____

_____

_____

Date

I AM GRATEFUL THAT THE EXTRAORDINARY POWER OF LOVE FILLS ALL OF MY INNER PARTS.

I am lifted from earth to heaven. I do all things but fail.

Date

Cecilia B. Loving

_____

_____

_____

_____

_____

_____

_____

_____

_____

_____

_____

_____

_____

_____

_____

_____

_____

_____

_____

_____

Date

I AM GRATEFUL THAT I SEE GOD SEEING ME.

My vision is restored.

Date

Cecilia B. Loving

_____

_____

_____

_____

_____

_____

_____

_____

_____

_____

_____

_____

_____

_____

_____

_____

_____

_____

Date

_____

_____

_____

_____

_____

_____

_____

_____

_____

_____

_____

_____

_____

_____

_____

_____

_____

_____

_____

_____

_____

Date

Cecilia B. Loving

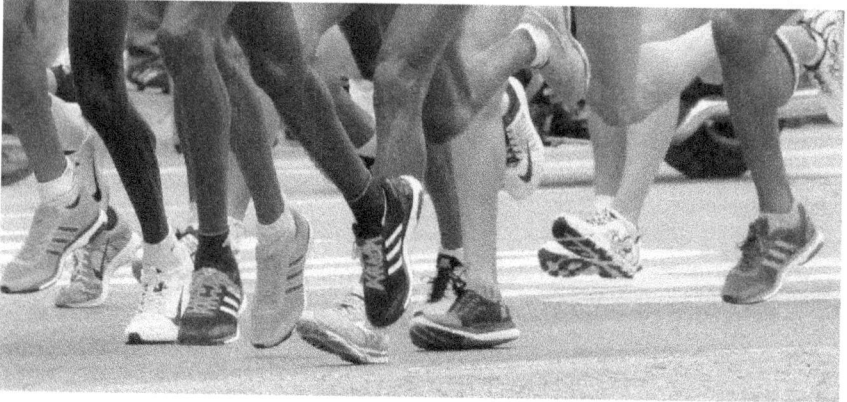

I SEE GOD IN THE ACCOMPLISHMENT OF MY GOALS

Date

ABOUT THE AUTHOR

Reverend Cecilia Loving is the spiritual leader of SPIRITMUV® (www.spiritmuv.com), a non-denominational church in New York City that embraces all faiths celebrating love for one another.

After practicing law for over 20 years, Rev. Loving also heeded her calling into the ministry through church and writing. Her first book, PRAYERS FOR THOSE STANDING ON THE EDGE OF GREATNESS, has already changed the lives of many. Her second book, GOD IS A BROWN GIRL TOO, is one of the first books in which God speaks as us to us. GOD IS A LAWYER TOO: TEN UNLIMITED LAWS OF SUCCESS is fiction and the first book in which Rev. Loving directly applies spiritual law to the work environment. Even though it takes place in a legal/corporate work environment, the principles of success are applicable to any walk of life. If you are looking to change your life to experience God's favor, all of these books will help you change your life. They can be purchased on Amazon.com or wherever books are sold.

Rev. Loving resides in Brooklyn, New York with her husband Rev. Marlon Cromwell.

myrtle
tree
press, LLC